Texas A&M University: It's Not Just a College, It's a Culture

by Tiffani Jaqua

Illustrated by
Cristobal Carselle

Jaqua Publishing

DEDICATION

To my boys, Darren and Bryson, I hope you always continue to learn and enrich your educations.

Acknowledgements

I would like to give special thanks to Hunter McLeod, art teacher extraordinaire, for introducing me to such a wonderful illustrator, Cristobal Carselle. He is an incredibly talented and remarkable young man. Cris, you continue to amaze me with your creativity, adaptability and easygoing nature when working together…twelve books together so far and counting. To my twin sister, Stephanie Hutchinson (also Fightin' Texas Aggie class of '90), I won't forget our fond memories at Texas A&M University together…especially in Leggett Hall.

Attending Texas A&M University will have you feeling larger-than-life,

You see, Aggies aren't just Aggies for four years, Aggies are Aggies for life!

The college was founded in 1871 as the Agricultural and Mechanical College knows as Texas A.M.C.,

And then became Texas A&M University, TAMU, in 1963.

Everywhere you go you'll feel the Aggie spirit, known as the "spirit of Aggieland",

And once you step foot on campus, you'll agree, it's the perfect alma mater for a school so grand.

It's known as the friendliest campus in the world. For instance, "Howdy" is the official greeting,

That's a word you'll say often...and to everyone you're meeting.

There are a few additional vocabulary terms you'll need to know, which you'll often hear,

For instance, "Whoop" represents excitement, although tradition permits it to be said only junior and/or senior year.

Good bull" is another term, which embraces the wonderful Aggie spirit,

It's used to show Aggie approval, so fairly often you will hear it.

"Gig 'em" is a term, represented by putting your right thumb in an upward position,

Making this gesture when you speak the term, has long been hailed tradition.

Football games at A&M are phenomenal, especially since Aggieland is "Home of the 12th Man",

This represents a willingness for Ags to serve when needed, so at games be ready to stand.

HOME OF THE 12th MAN

You see Aggies support the players during games, so Aggies do not sit,

This is a non-negotiable for Aggies, unless injured, so you'll need to commit.

The 12ᵗʰ Man tradition began in 1922 when E. King Gill stepped up to play in the game, allowing the injured team to be unimpeded,

And The 12ᵗʰ Man spirit is still evident today, encouraging Ags to always step up, when needed.

Hats left on during yells is considered rude, so if you leave yours on you might hear this,

"Uncover!" or "Hat's off!" or even the infamous Aggie "hissssss".

UNCOVER!

During games school spirit is led by five yell leaders, who are selected by the student body,

They rally students and support the team...and everything you'd want school spirit to embody.

Midnight yell practice is held on Friday nights before each home game for students to review each yell,

So that when yell leaders pass signals back in the stadium during games, students know each yell well.

Each time Aggies score a touchdown, the canon will fire sounding loud, like a gunshot,

Tradition encourages Ags to kiss their dates after each score, but if you're alone, then not.

Texas A&M University is steeped in tradition and is the home of "The Fightin' Texas Aggie Band",

With marching performances so spectacular, your unwavering attention they'll command.

They're the largest military band in the United States and perform during half-time on Kyle Field,

You might even have an opportunity to experience the famous "Block T" formation revealed.

At the conclusion of each game, the Aggie War Hymn is sung whether the Ags lost or won,

It's fondly known as Hullabaloo, Caneck-Caneck and was written during World War 1.

The lyrics include "saw Varsity's horns off" which is in regards to another college...A&M's long-standing rivalry,

It's about removing the horns from the other school's longhorn mascot, you see.

The Corps of Cadets is the oldest student organization on campus, which has been voluntary since 1965,

They're knows as "keepers of the spirit" and "the guardians of tradition". They keep Aggie spirit alive.

Each level of cadets has uniform differences. Seniors wear boots which provides them a bit more clout,

But all corps uniforms are worn with school spirit and pride, which is what Texas A&M's all about.

Ross Volunteers (RV) is the military escort of the governor of Texas and the honor guard of Texas A&M Corps of Cadets,

The Ross Volunteer Company also performs at various events for fallen Aggies, so those students no none forgets.

Although Sarge is an image identified with Texas A&M, the "First Lady of Aggieland" is Reveille,

She's the official mascot of TAMU and a very special breed of dog, the Collie.

She's the highest ranking member of the Corps of Cadets, and she's absolutely adored,

Her Company E-2 handler, the Mascot Corporal, takes her to classes, but class is dismissed when she barks...meaning she's bored.

Planted over one hundred years ago near the Academic Building you'll find Century Tree,

It's rumored marriages will last forever, if proposals occur under its branches, down on one knee.

Elephant Walk, originating in 1926, is another unique tradition, honoring seniors getting ready to graduate,

It happens annually before each final home football game, preparing seniors to acclimate.

Students link their hands to shoulders in a single file line as they celebrate this event with their senior classmates,

Remembering campus life and sharing memories before graduation and everything that further awaits.

The Aggie ring is one of the best known traditions. It's been mostly unchanged since 1933,

Aggies get their rings on Ring Day, and during commencement, rings are turned outward for all to see.

You see, Texas A&M University is a school based on traditions with an Aggie code of honor to follow,

The astounding pride you feel being a student on campus will certainly not leave you feeling hollow.

Aggieland is grounded in unique traditions that make Texas A&M University more than just another school,

It's, undeniably, the culture and spirit at Aggieland, which leaves all other colleges appearing quite miniscule.

Tiffani Jaqua

Tiffani Jaqua

Find the definitions for any vocabulary words you don't know on this page. A few vocabulary words are listed below.

acclimate—

cadets—

embody—

gesture—

mascot—

phenomenal—

rally—

tradition—

steeped—

unimpeded-

List any other new vocabulary words you discovered.

1.

2.

3.

4.

5.

6.

7.

8.

9.

10.

Imagine you're the illustrator and draw your own pictures of your favorite Texas A&M University traditions or experiences.

List sets of rhyming words you found in this book.
Ex.) <u>Reveille</u> and <u>Collie</u>

1.

2.

3.

4.

5.

6.

7.

8.

9.

10.

ABOUT THE AUTHOR

Tiffani Jaqua (pronounced Jakeway) is a Texas A&M University graduate...Fightin' Texas Aggie class of '90. She has worked in education and counseling for nearly thirty years. She is widowed and lives with her two sons in The Woodlands, Texas. This is her thirteenth children's book. Her inspiration for this book stems from fond memories as a resident advisor and student at Texas A&M University in College Station.

ABOUT THE ILLUSTRATOR

Cristobal Carselle is a young artist, recent high school graduate and aspiring illustrator based in Houston, Texas. He has been drawing and painting for nearly a decade. He has received many awards for his work. This is his twelfth illustrated book with Tiffani Jaqua and he plans on working on many more projects.

If you enjoyed this book, check out Tiffani Jaqua's other books, available at Amazon.

<u>Blowing Dandelions with Sea Lions</u> (2018) A collection of 54 rhyming poems and illustrations on various topics

<u>It's My Turn in the Front Seat</u> (2020) A collection of 54 rhyming poems and illustrations on various topics

<u>The Students in Room 109</u> (2020) A collection of 54 rhyming poems and illustrations on various topics

<u>Questions for Santa</u> (2021) A rhyming poetry/activity book about all things Santa Claus related

<u>Questions for the Easter Bunny</u> (2021) A rhyming poetry/activity book about all things Easter Bunny related

<u>Questions for the Tooth Fairy</u> (2021) A rhyming poetry/activity book about all things Tooth Fairy related

<u>Halloween Things</u> (2021) A rhyming poetry/activity book about Halloween related topics

<u>Traveling Around the World</u> (2021) A rhyming poetry/activity book about locations around the world and traveling

<u>Distinctively Diverse Dinosaurs</u> (2021) A rhyming poetry/activity book about dinosaur facts

<u>Phases of the Moon</u> (2021) A rhyming poetry/activity book about the eight phases of the lunar cycle

<u>Phenomenally Pragmatic Penguins</u> (2021) A rhyming poetry/activity book about penguin facts

<u>Questions for the Leprechaun</u> (2022) A rhyming poetry/activity book about all things St. Patrick's Day related

Texas A&M University: It's Not Just a College, It's a Culture

Made in the USA
Monee, IL
26 July 2022

7d1302e9-32ca-4704-8462-f8786e3ef4e0R02